THE INDIA GRANDPA HAS NEVER SEEN

THE INDIA GRANDPA HAS NEVER SEEN

Hrushikesh Mallick

Translated by
Ramesh Patnaik
and
Harekrushna Das

BLACK EAGLE BOOKS
2020

BLACK EAGLE BOOKS
USA address:
7464 Wisdom Lane
Dublin, OH 43016

India address:
E/312, Trident Galaxy, Kalinga Nagar,
Bhubaneswar-751003, Odisha, India

E-mail: info@blackeaglebooks.org
Website: www.blackeaglebooks.org

First International Edition Published by
BLACK EAGLE BOOKS, 2020

The India Grandpa Has Never Seen
by **Hrushikesh Mallick**
Translated by **Ramesh Patnaik** and **Harekrushna Das**

Original Copyright © **Hrushikesh Mallick**
Translation Copyright © **Ramesh Patnaik** and **Harekrushna Das**

All rights reserved. No part of this publication may be reproduced, stored in a retrieval system, or transmitted, in any form or by any means, electronic, mechanical, photocopying, recording or otherwise without the prior permission of the publisher.

Cover & Interior Design: Ezy's Publication

ISBN- 978-1-64560-079-4 (Paperback)
Library of Congress Control Number: 2020939297

Printed in United States of America

To
Sharmistha & Brahmaprakash

Foreword

I remember meeting Hrushikesh Mallick at National Poets' Meet in Bharat Bhavan, Bhopal as a fiery young man. (Ah, I was young too!) Though I could follow his poems only through translations, which is the case even now, I could see that his poetry was unlike most Odia poetry I was exposed to: full of wistfulness, nostalgia and nature still standing green despite human impermanence. His poetry, I could then sense, was no-nonsense and down to earth. Plus like the poetry of another contemporary Odia poet-friend Soubhagya Kumar Mishra, Mallick's poetry was not monologues but dialogic. Dialogic and down to earth: this is how I would still characterize Mallick's poetry a very longtime after my first encounter with it.

Further it has several attributes which make it an illustration of what Pablo Neruda called Impure Poetry. From the viewpoint of the man standing in the street, on the farm or plantations, or in the pristine jungles threatened by the demon of progress, Mallick's poetry makes us participate in the trials and tribulations of the oppressed sections of the society forcing us to listen and be attentive to 'the still, sad music of humanity."

While trying to empathize with oppressed men and women, Mallick also steers clear of the danger of lapsing into shouts and slogans of so called revolutionary poetry.

With his keen eye for truth, he points out how even revolution can degenerate into a deadly business. His poetry looks at sorrows and sufferings inflicted by men on men and women from diverse angles and through different personae, which lends his poetry an epic scale. However, it purges the epic of its conservative contents and breathes an air of savage realism into it.

I hope that the present English translation of his widely acclaimed poetry collection 'Jeje Dekhi Nathiba Bharat' (The India Grandpa Has Never Seen) will introduce the readers into the little known areas and the unchartered areas of Indian poetry in Odia.

The translators have on the whole succeeded in mapping out Odia into English idioms.

I wish the book great success.

H.S. Shivaprakash
Director, The Tagore Centre, Berlin &
Former Professor of Theatre Studies, JNU, New Delhi

Translator's Apologia

Hrushikesh Mallick is one of the veteran poets of our times. He has been in the forefront of neo-modern literary movement of the 21st century Odisha. His poetry still retains the last strains of classicism post-Independence and the cadence reflecting modernity. A scholar, teacher and journalist Hrushikesh Mallick is also an Odisha Sahitya Akademi award winner for his compilation of poems titled Dhana Saunta Jhia.

The current anthology Jeje Dekhinathiba Bharat which won him the coveted Sarala Sahitya Award is rich in Romantic essence that transports the readers into our pastoral origins in which modern India is deeply entrenched. Hrushikesh essays to explore through poetry the spirit of Mother India that reminds its children of the core values for which the geo-political map stands as a mute testimony. The scheme of symbolism the poet adopts is intricate because of the ethnic quality he invests in the emotions through agrarian imagery.

The rural rituals, customs and myths surrounding poverty in the countryside is peculiarly Indian. This is precisely why we chose to translate poet Hrushikesh. The portrait of India in terms of its emotions encompassing the quality of life and the degeneration of human values in the hands of a chosen few is awe-inspiring.

We are not sure whether we have done justice to the poet's work of art. At times, we got stuck for days with a couple of words coined by the poet himself; thanks to his passion for invention. We urge him to pardon us for trying to fathom the creator's masterpiece with our little wisdom and shallow understanding of his ingenuity.

Ramesh Patnaik
Harekrushna Das

Hide and Seek

I do not remember when I began my fascination with the words; nor can I ever remember it. Nor do I know when it will come to an end. My "Samskar" taught me to dovetail letters of the alphabet, and shroud them with different signs to make "words", and transform them into "parts of speech". It bestowed upon me a certain trove of "meanings" as my initial treasure. And said, " Even though you start playing with only this much, you will gradually discover a lot of new "meanings." As your play intensifies to get transformed into a meditation, you'll certainly be transported to somewhere beyond the horizon of "meanings."

While playing with words right since my adolescent days, it suddenly occurred to me that it was not merely a game; but something more than that: "a Divine Play." Words fight with words in this Divine Play, and their reverberation mesmerises the readers. Sometimes as a sullenness and sometimes as an embrace it manifests itself with its manifold meanings and signification; sometimes in a sonorous voice, and sometimes with subdued humility.

Once upon the moonlit village granary, "words" provoked me, "Let's play the game of hide and seek; I'll seek when you go hiding, and you'll find as I hide myself."

We were both players and spectators of that game. I have since then been searching for inner-consciousness of "words" along the path of my journey punctuated with pauses and unsteady movements. I have sometimes been able to find it, and at other times I have failed to catch even a glimpse of it. While trying to touch it there at the other side of the corn-pile, it has overtaken me to touch the winning-mark. I remain the very same thief, always as ever. "Meaning" has drifted away from me.

It has sometimes come to my clutches on its own. Unravelling itself and transporting me to the realm beyond the clouds and stars, it has made me victorious; has confessed to be the "thief"- the loser.

But it is more secretive than it is manifest; it has a lot more yet to be unraveled. I often wonder whether poetry has been writing me or I have been writing poetry since the days it took me under its spell. "Just as the farmer searches for the bullock after he has lost it (Bhisma Parva-Sarala Mahabharata), I have frantically been searching everywhere for the "meaning" that always slips beyond the vision even though it creates an illusion of being visible; searching in the solitary cornfields of "meaning"; crossing the borders of the fields, beyond the birth, surpassing even death!

Dear readers! I have made my "Prarabdha" (Destiny) as the playground of my game of hide and seek; made "words" my companion of Divine Play; and made solitude my commitment. Can you hear this Divine Proclamation of poetry? Has the word-play of any poet ever been successful leaving aside your "Yes" or "No" ?

Hrushikesh Mallick

Contents

The India Grandpa Has Never Seen	15
How Taila Sees Nation	17
A Dream of an Employee	19
I'm a Mao-Cadre (I)	21
I'm a Mao-Cadre (II)	24
I Complete Forty-Seven (I)	26
I Complete Forty-Seven (II)	28
Swineherd	30
Today is your Birthday Maa	32
Helpless Law-Book	34
Reminiscence	36
Call of War	38
New Year Celebration	40
Deceptive Echoes	42
Epilogue	44
A Weaver's Song	47
Ode to Winter	48
Won't Talk of Revolution*	51
Gobaraghati-I	54
Gobaraghati-II	56
A Word on the Horizon	58
Kandulana	61
Naxalite Girl	64
Immersion	67
Today is the Rally	69
Diary of a Betel-Vineyard Farmer	71
Diary of a Courtesan	73
Couplets of Rebellion	75
Shame on that Nation	77
Jhunu Garg	79
Tsunami-1	83
Tsunami: 2	86
Missing Village	89
Nickname For a Daughter	91
The Matter Is...	93
Rain-Drenched	96
A Son's Letter to Father	99
Tribute to Hetal	102
No-Devakee	105
Nithari	108
Imrana, For You...	111

The India Grandpa
Has Never Seen

Did you really go out
In that rally to Bhubaneswar, Grandpa?
Asked the grandson
Coming back from a tour.

: "Oh, yes." Smiled the old man.
"Where did you put up?"
:"A legislator's den", Grandpa replied.
"And, about your grub?"
:"Crude rice, prawn-dal mix,
Country tomato gravy..."recounts the old man.

"How did you commute?" the grandson was agog.
: "Aye, simple. Boarded Tuku Babu's truck"
"Tuku, who's this soul?"
: "Chema, the oil miller's son.
He is no more that old Tuku
Whose early life spent in poverty;
Now, owns a fleet of trucks and buses.
Be the ministers or officers-
They queue up at his residence
To meet him."

Where else did you visit, and
What did you see? Asked the boy
With enthusiasm.

Went to Konark and watched
Kumkum Mohanty dance
Went to Puri and saw sculpture
Falling off temple, hordes
Of leaders crowding Canteen Square
Of speeches and sit-ins.

Heaving a sigh of relief
The grandson reclined for a while
On a pillow, just as the Over-aged God
Had sheltered Himself amid the wild Shiali-shrubs
At the end of the Dwapara era:
And queried; "Didn't you see Grandpa, in Konark
A Dharama staggering in intoxication;
The same rogue who disrobed a tourist girl
Last afternoon?
Did you ever find the mutt- vicar
At Purushottam, accused
Of appalling crimes, and still at large?
Liquor-laden trucks passing by
The Cola company in Mancheswar
Likes winging Dola chariots?
And did you see under the mattress
Currency wads bearing Gandhi's head,
Or smuggled guns??"

How Taila Sees Nation

For Taila
His anguished motherland dangles
From the corners of
Your ravenous teeth
You've dragged her rapaciously
Like a corpse
On highway.

For Taila,
His Motherland is a tiny nest:
A roof under the fearless sky
A fistful of coarse rice
Lumped up in the plate,
Of a family members
Happily sharing their foods

For Taila,
His motherland is abound with
Rare produce of forests,
Shower across the skies
Over lush green hills
Fragrance of leaves permeating
The palms with crystal clear water
Pouring in their fold.

For Taila,
His motherland is
A people's call at your doorstep
Where no one returns empty hands
And with a desperate heart;
Patriotism, for him, is to be able
To borrow a palm-full of salt from a neighbor;
Nation for him is a heaven where
Even the crazy wind won't dare to touch
The veils of the willful country-maidens;
Motherland for him is
To respond a call for help-
Be it from the valleys of Kashmir
Or from the ways to Amarnath;

For Taila,
Motherland is
To get mesmerized
In the cheering songs of life
Before the locusts devour everything;
To become a beau
With the blossom of a flower, and
Become a martyr
Embracing the first pellet
To keep atop the motherland.

■

A Dream of an Employee

It's no issue whether you get
Paid today or tomorrow:
They should at least announce
On newspaper or in television,
You could borrow some money:
What more can you hope to do?

You needn't show off
Your fake vanities before son
For gulping your pocket money
"Stupid fellow, sans grades!"

With a raise, you may ask kid:
"Wanna rigorous coaching?"
Never mind cost, my son!

Needn't scream at wife
With virile superiority:
"You base woman –
Don't you know
Gandhiji himself washed
His clothes at Sabarmati?"

Rather cajole her: "Honey,
We'll go for washing machine

When cash flows,
I know, you're tired of it.
You may walk with your head
Held high before shopkeeper
That turned down your son
From lending ration;
You can now shop anywhere
If you had the means!

It's nice to snub Mr. Ray:
Salute him when he lands
With your left hand,
Ask him to find a groom
For daughter from noble tree,
But not a con contractor!

It's no issue whether you get
Paid or not; may the merciful government
Announce on television or in papers
In its mellowed voice:
"Empty coffers will swell soon;
Dear employees, endure!
Until elections."

■

I'm a Mao-Cadre (I)

Come to the point
Answer me straight
Rivers 'n' hills are
Not your inheritance
That you can gift them
At your will
To the corporate and traders
Stay careful-
The gun I wield is always ready:
I'm a Maoist.

Nothing is your own.
The chair you've occupied,
Is mine: the dams you've built over rivers
Are mine.
The forests you've destroyed
Are Mine
The floating tenders are mine.
The *Mahula* and its spirit you plunder
From my forests are also mine.

You have made it your wont
To bargain for human lives,
Their soul and their freedom;
You've hushed up the voice

Of our parents and elders with bribe
And usurped the chair
You now claim as your own.
You've devoured like caterpillar
Everything we considered our life.
You've spoilt our life
Playing with our emotion for years;
But beware!
I'm now a Maoist.

You've only seen my mask
But not the self that rebels.
Through deception of showering help
You've seduced me to your honeymoon.
Abducting from my father's lap
You've sold me to a pimp.
Dangling a bait of living-wage before her
You've toyed with my sister
Like a lecher.

My life has turned pallid, justas
My hairs are dry and raised
Lacking nourishment of oil, and
My moustache looks haggard
Like a blade of grass.
With my tottering stand
Like a bush in the desert-
I'm famished and lusterless.

It's no tears, there's dynamite
Under my skin keen to explode...
I'm an acid that burns your law-books:
I cannot be contained in them.

No prison of yours
Can keep me captive for long,
Their walls crumble into pieces
With a touch of my arms.
Wild crackers of Diwali I am
That can blow away even your
Concrete roofs.

I'll now drop off like spittle
On the pious platter of your opulent dishes, and
Dangle like a chopped off head
From the slender neck
Of your curvaceous dancing belle.
I cannot be enslaved anywhere in land,
Nor in water or in dump
Neither in space…
As I'm the knell of a cataclysm
And a seedling of anew order:
I am a Mao Cadre!

I'm a Mao-Cadre(II)

Why do you fume
If I blew up a railway track
Or torched a police station?
Why raise a storm of anger
If I detonated khaki-jeeps
Using landmines?
No big deals these are;
but like the fun games of a kid.

You'll now witness the real game:
I'll become Rudra
Atop Kailash snow peaks
You'll hear thunderbolts
Strike down from skies…
I'll pierce like lightning
Into your veins and blood;
I may even demand sacrifice
Of an infant or a pregnant woman's life
Standing furious on the horizon;
If need be tear apart the flag
To wrap up the bleeding genital
Of a bruised minor
You've deserted along
The edge of a forest road
After ravishing her like a brute.

I'll even uproot and fetch
Mountains that grow medicines
If at all a wound remains unhealed;
Fling sovereignty of the nation
Out for auction
If ever a human remains
Impoverished and unfed.

I'll die fighting
I'll fight even while dying,
An ultra, unconquerable:
I'm Time and End Times.
I know more than you do
The magical art of survival.

I'll show up from anywhere
While hiding
I'll fade away from view
Even when you behold me
Remember-
I am a Mao Cadre..!!!

I Complete Forty-Seven (I)

Nothing in this life
Could be completed yet,
Even though I complete forty-seven...!

Myriad thoughts crowd up memory
Like winter birds from Siberia
Nesting in Chilika:
Where should our daughter study-
Utkal or Hyderabad?
Will it be too early to quit job? Or
Right to enter politics?
Was President Kalam right
Singing songs with children
And break the protocol?

Yet,
College forms get exhausted
In banks due to delays
In mopping up cash:
Son grows up taller like Sal tree,
And groom for daughter
Might be on his way

Can't move out of home
Or into town due to
Stiff waist and joints;
As I complete forty-seven
My dawns swiftly turn
Into dusks.

I Complete Forty-Seven (II)

Before I venture out
My veggie bag pops out
To fetch provisions home,
But I miss something
Every time I go to bring.

Household burdens
Squeeze themselves up into my house;
No, it's rather my home
That the bard Madhusudan
Likened to Heaven.

Often during a morning walk
I philosophize to Kalpanta:
"Is one's home really his own?
Nothing is ours
When we die;
Let's visit then Chandaneswar..."

I fondle the kid in her arms, and
Ask my neighbour:
"Do you get pure milk
Or adulterated with water?"

I walk with unsteady steps
Along with my haggard shadow
I stop and flounder;
There's none when I look back,

But someone very close
Reminds me: I complete forty-seven,
I grow old.

Swineherd

Banchha as they address him
Lives in a crippling nothingness.
Sky a top is his roof,
The earth under his feet,
Sun 'n' Moon are his lamps,
And wind, his ceiling fan.

Holding a drum made of water gourd
He keeps walking from daybreak
Till Sunset when four directions
Keep stretching their horizon.

A herd of pigs has been his only asset
Since the days India attained freedom.
Many like Gandhi came and disappeared
But Banchha remains the same swineherd.

He owns a passel of hogs today,
Driving his parcel of pigs into puddle
Banchha relaxes on ridge
Spreading his dhoti

Visualizing a distant history
Of anonymous, God-forsaken land
Through wild shrubs

Where hills and streams
Aren't entangled in politics.

His slim teenage girl
Goes vending ribbon, necklace
And nail polish
In the country side;
Wife borrows curries
From neighbourhood;
Banchha passes his days, months
Playing his water gourd-drum.

On a fine morning Banchha finds
Concrete buildings on water bodies:
Wind bears no aroma of flowers,
No more the gloom in clouds
He used to see in his childhood.
Faded in the fumes
Of factory chimneys
Lusterless appears
The ivory-moon.

His home bears no trace
Of wife whose saree lies on floor;
Daughter's frock ripped off the buttons
Hanging on clothesline;
The herd of swine missing;
Only their tiny tails wagging in the distant fog.

Banchha was heard no more:
But a few reported seeing him yesterday
For the last time in the evening!

Today is your Birthday Maa

It is your birthday Maa
A cuckoo's call
 Delights my ears
When mango orchard
Permeates flowery aromas
Greeting honeybees;
Is it time for me
To go on an invasion
Riding a stallion?

What's this Maa!
The earth grew fainter
The sky colourless
Moonlit horizon distraught
With the loss.
As you advance your feet
Towards throne,
Thorny bushes and wild plums
Spread a blanket of illusion.

Did they chop off your feet
That stood on earth
For you could wear
Filigree anklets of Cuttack?
Should you console me in sickness, despair

And massage my forehead
With your warm hands-
Did they remove your hands
That were west wind
In heat wave ?

Did they pluck your tongue
Lest you should cajole me when I trip?

You were born today mom,
Getting her leave granted
From manager of a tea garden
The young worker's wife buys perfume
From cheap provisions stores in Assam;
Trying to fulfill wishes of Biluakhai,
The daily wager of Surat might be
Playing the dice of life...
Stuffing envelopes with hopes and dreams
Of connecting earth with the sky:
The betel shop keeper of Indupur
May be writing letters
Sitting exultant in Kolkata.

Helpless Law-Book

Law will take its own course,
Says Minister; while cops say:
Lo, here's clinching evidence!

Prosecutor's first witness
Claims accused had a dagger;
Second says on oath
He can identify the accused,
As third claims he's eyewitness!

Defence lawyer grills typically:
How long was the dagger?
Are you sure the man you identify
Is the real culprit? Did he put on
A brown lungi or a black?

Responses go wrong
In the courtroom.
The judge warns of order,
But the accused gets acquitted.

You take oath on Scripture,
Pledge to protect
Truth:

The advocate's white necktie,
Black coat on the judge,
And a glittering
Ashokan emblem on the table of the judge
Symbolise justice

After the court adjourns-
The judge stares vacantly
At the camera,
Lawyers greet each other outside:
The acquitted criminal
Ridicules the constable
To keep his hand-cuffs away.
Helpless law-book laments with a sigh:
"Relieve me of the helplessness
Of being born as mere letters,
Salvage me from fetters, My God!"

Reminiscence

I'm at the Ninth Floor Complex
With pager in hand, and mobile phone
In my trouser pocket.
What does still haunt me then?
The memories of my village?

Mom waters the roots of Bel tree
With her wet saree on,
Sister-in-law stirs milk,
With a coconut-shell ladle,
Dad rivets wooden handle to shovel,
And uncle's younger son
With his legs stretched in the backyard
Recites school poem
About Ranjeet Singh astride his horse...

Roasting of leaf-wrapped *Mahurali* fish
On pyre; aroma of new rice
Steaming from clay pots in my village
Permeates here the lanes of this city.

It's raining there on Television,
In front of the screen
Sits glued the naughty son;
'What's *Kesur* plant Dad,'
Queries daughter, my fond child.

I've pizza on my platter:
I still reminisce the rice
Fried on clay pan
Standing atthe nine-storied
Heads of department building
With pager in my hand...

(*Mahurali* : A type of small fresh water fish)

■

Call of War

When you command:
"Attention", they're alert;
Say "arms down", they put weapons down.
You do everything whimsically, though
You aren't the globe's master!

You haven't painted this Sunrise
Nor Sunset is your creation,
These stars and planets, hills and woods
Aren't under your sway.
Nor did you compose the bees' humming,
Neither moonlit night,
Nor the blue lilies!

The melody of flute should reverberate
On rural outskirts at dusk,
Ajan at mosque, bells at temple
Should mesmerize the soul, but
"Bomb!" You said at Sunset, and
They bombarded!

Angels should descend from hilltop
To lake at night
Strolling on solitary pathways, and

Goddesses burn glowworm wicks, but
Who set fire on gunpowder
At such moments?

Before cops apprehend the accused, they
Should have checked at home:
If there's a child or a villain
Who's dug a bunker for Alibaba
And his gang of forty!

You're a mastermind
With a different name
Who has snatched a doll
Or a slate-piece, giving calls for Jehad; and
Kicking away the kitchenware
Made a clamour for ration.

The sky built its bedspread
For birds to flock together,
Riverbed for kids to float kites: but
Everywhere your shouting mikes
In the plea of prayers or 'namaj';
Everywhere the terror of cruise,
And the thunder of gun fire!

Lights will switch on when you command,
Put off as you desire, though
You aren't the sole master of this soil.

■

New Year Celebration

(I)
How did the New Year party go?
With songs, dance and champagne?
Didn't you go to Hadgarh for picnic?

Heard, your emigrant uncle
Breathed his last on way.
Hope, it's a rumour.
Nothing more to pen down:
Nothing is fine, my lady's
Rheumatism getting worse
And son has fractured his left leg
After a bad fall from scooter.

(II)
Didn't you read papers?
Nine-year-old gang raped
Before being bludgeoned to death?
She was Sangeeta of Standard III,
The child you had pampered with
A cup of ice-cream
At Vedavyas mela;
Don't you remember?

Ah! The poor girl couldn't have
Wept or screeched, as
They would've gagged her hard.

If at all she screamed,
How could anyone hear her wail
Amidst nasty filmy-numbers,
Speeches, and horselaugh of villains,
Celebrations marking anniversary of the government,
And opposition booming calls for rally…!

(III)
We went on information
Saw her blood clotting
On her temple, skull and genitals, and
Torn out cotton panties.
Her frock sucked by honeybees,
Her flowers on plait disheveled...

Sangeeta didn't respond to anybody,
Not even to her mom
Who had accompanied her
A little while ago in an errand!

Nothing goes well since then,
No sleep even though I lie in couch,
No hunger at lunch time.
Publishers call for poems
But poetry goes for a nap.

Methinks, I'll quit writing:
Of what use is writing poetry
For twenty years that fails to protect
A young girl from being mauled
By a herd of bison!

Deceptive Echoes

Man, Oh dear Man
I called aloud-
The echo deceives me
My darling child is playing in forest
Toying the tiger.

Are you awake or asleep?
Are you dead or alive?

Priest, Fakir and Father- they call you
All crimes are condoned
If at all they call you human-
Even petty sins are condemned.

Humans are mere gudgeon fish
Your fires are ready to bake;
Staring from your lusty swing
You enjoy deaths as though a cake.

In a moon-blanched night
With a wight as you traversed;
To bring even the heaven down
You had us promised;
But in place of giving thingummies
Everything you snatched.

Ration prices soar high
But value of life falls;
One firmament for endless stars
But a million religions (!) appalls.

Many Kandhamals keep burning
Nation callously espies;
Ah! Killer slumber grapples the sentry
Vultures hover around Godhra skies;
His poems suffer glaucoma
Even though the poet boasts.

Tongue seems locked, and
Rose in hands of a bear;
Graveyard gulf mutts, and
Mom douses son's pyre;
Look! Street plays turn wars, and
Deceptive echoes scare.

Epilogue

Who are you walking
In the feeble light
Along concrete pathways?

It's Trinath Behera of Nayagarh
Lives in Kargil slum
I'm professional thug
Is your papa fine?

Doomed with his throat cancer
And still smoking grass
After mom's demise in ascites.

Who's there like the lone star
Shining along horizon
On a new moon night?

I'm Hasna Roy, call me Hasi.
Hometown Gop in Puri district.
What are you here for?
I'm selling out to darkness
The aroma of tender corns;
The hearth lies doused at home,
And mom crippled with arthritis.

The flyover is depopulated
Like the deserted wedding pandal,
The wobbling moon about to set:
Who's this tipsy man? Kanha?
How's life at Bengaluru?
What's your pay now?

I lost my job, the girl ditched me,
And sister's alliance got broken.
Jasmine smiles of fiancée
In corporate cabins
Louder than bellow of buffaloes
Shrilling whistles of trains.
Innocence writ in drawing books, and
Dollar dreams
Get you glued to the chair
From neck to knee.

Nominal interest on loans lure,
Bush and Chidambaramon hoardings,
And ours is hand-to-mouth life:
Wear a little, sleep a while
And cast your vote,
Hold up traffic, vandallise mutt
Or torch a church.
Grow up lonely
Like basil plant at graveyard,
You are the friend; you are the slogan,
Thumb impression, knife, BPL
And lifetime mobile phone.

You are sleep, weep and all groan
Half-consumed black berries you are, and

You are the blinking bats -
A temple priest, Hasna, Kanha,
Trinath and long-forgotten Gayatri,
Who fade into oblivion
With the going of the world...
You are the darkness
You are the earth!

■

A Weaver's Song

Vaisakh in mid-summer
Is opportune time for wild hen
To rewrite lyrics or inspire
Simulee blossoms.

Ration rice and dal elude poor
When pet cats slumber in hearth.
Generous are our masters
That sport Khadi outfits
Sans handloom spools, and
Target blindfold even swimming fish
Reflected in water.

Black melons are pink within
Stone apples are bombs above;
Jobless brands knife and dagger
Don't play cards or dice anymore;

Tender foot walk on fire
As they quench flames of hunger.
Laws drafted in reams
Pleas fall on deaf ears of officers;
Juice kiosks mushroom wayside,
Clay pots smile with holes underneath
Happiness jostles in illusions,
Shattered dreams won't fetch alms!

Ode to Winter

Come this way, O' Winter
Did you rush through Kandhamal
Hills abound in turmeric canopy
My dad nurtures those plants.

Didn't you see the sulking girl
On a culvert on the village edge?
Do you think her elder sibling Rajani
Will ever come back home?

Time is a great deceiver:
No more before us is the happiness
Of our younger days;
How can we find a way out?
All are victims of predicament!

Men propose
But regime disposes,
Look at the fellowmen around:
All are but conmen.

Why do you appear dazed,
Are you okay physically?

Why look disillusioned
Like loop less scripts
On suicide note of the girl
Who hanged herself?

How so much the modest housemaid
May try to decorate-
City is city;
It lacks the fragrance of village.

Despite simple pathways
Babus beautify human habitats
With plants on lawns
Dahlia and exotic Dianthus
You remember how shrubs on pond hedges
Bloom moonflowers with fragrance
And mom will ignore them:
"Don't go near, snakes creep around".

Like a labourer's undaunted spirits
Dandelions raise their beaks
Amid wild bushes
Patting the hybrid marigold
Laxmi enters granary, and
Deity Saraswati steps inside the sanctorum.
Had they inhaled the aroma
Of bonfire-baked brinjals,
Would anyone ever torch
Schools, colleges, temples
Or mosques over trivia?

I continue to blabber,
And you gaping fool

Loiter outside home…
I heard auntie's tale
In childhood while drowsing; but
You've heard it the whole Winter!

The cow goes back to forest
Honestly after feeding its calf;
Tell me: was there the tiger
Waiting to prey upon her?

Won't Talk of Revolution

Night long tears of man,
Who had supported
A ridge gourd creeper,
Have percolated into his banyan
He couldn't fetch rotten brinjal
For his wife on family way.

Drug-addict his younger son
Has gone to discotheque;
May come back any time
Smelling of someone's deodorant
With borrowed clothes on.

Want me to speak of revolution?
Now listen…

Visibly, it's the mud verandah
Of Bira Bisoyi
Who departed in wee hours
Shouting Gandhi slogans all night;
Time has shrouded him
In the moss, of dead leaves.

Go, and enquire
Whether the sick widow

Got pension of her husband
Martyred in riots.

History never remembers Ali,
As the cunning inheritors treasure the
Emperor's seamless wine-glassware,
Baldpate of King George V
Or torso of Kanishka...
The crazy time finds space for it all.
Banyan used for hanging
Conceals itself a myriad times
As bonsai in the legs of chair.
Shrewd leaders
In plea of work forget
Birthday of *Birsa Munda**
Considering him of no use.
You want me to speak of revolution:
Now pay heed, and listen!

Flickering monsoon steps up
On stripped off hills
And goes back hurriedly
After a shower;
Just as a baby sucks
Its mom's voluptuous bosom-
The starving soil
Looks wistfully at
Grey clouds at distant sky.
But,
There'll be ample rain this time,
Never mind, assured Minister
In State Assembly.

Join us now to sing
The first number of free India:
Janagana Mana Adhinayak....
Come on Kids: we'll in both hands
All the balloons at the fair into air.

Come on pals,
We'll sleep tonight
For all our sleepless years!
You asked me to speak of revolution, but
Pardon me my country-men; I couldn't
Talk of our valour!!

Birsa Munda: A tribal freedom fighter hanged by the British rulers.

Gobaraghati-I

In darkness resembling unkempt hairs-
Drowned are the farmland,
Meadows and hamlets.
Like chain of dim neon lights
Hung from walls after the wedding-
Stars disperse through the wintry sky.
And, who's this block
On the nocturnal hour midway
With blinking headlights
Of company car?
Doesn't budge an inch
Despite persistent honking!

That's Mithu Munda;figured out the officer.
His maxilla
Still like splinter of porcupine
As it was in 1998;
Spear eyes of Dina Diggal
Haven't changed a bit;
Wiry hairs of
The childless widow, Para,
Like the lightning-ravaged sky
Still looks the same
As it used to be in 1998.
The officer now sure in conclusion:
It's Gobarghati.

Mustering up courage
Told the officer,
"Clear my ways, Gobaraghati!
Don't you see the rows of houses
The company built for
The people it evicted?
Didn't it build schools for your kids?
And hospital for better care?
Didn't provide jobs
For your unemployed youth?
So what, if a few
Still suffer from minor ailments, and
Move about still jobless?"

Now responded Gobarghati in pain;
"Of course the company
Has done a lot, Sir:
Has pumped bullets
Into hungry hundreds;
Severed our palms
When we lifted spades;
Gave a few decimals
As homestead land,
And tile-roofed stray huts
In the meadows.
They promised employment
For the jobless who ended up
In the dust of crusher units!"

■

N.B: A steel company evicted several hundred residents of Kalinganagar in 1998 to rehabilitate them at Gobarghati. The promises made to the oustees by the Government and the company authorities have been conveniently forgotten after usurping their land.

Gobaraghati- II

The night inches ahead
Through heated debates
That got clumsier.
Each word of his
Rebuffed by Gobarghati,
The officer faces resistance
Just as clouds struggle with the moon
To dominate the skies, or
Union leaders and the government
Confront across the table
Negotiating the demands.

"Gobarghati!" Shouted the officer,
"The company has delivered
Everything it had pledged:
Superfine roads, bright BPL lamps,
Polio-drops, and nursery rhymes for kids…

The company could create
At a command of the government
Effulgent moonlit nights
For the lilies of your wetlands;
Vernal wood effusing fragrance
Of ripe Bel fruits;
Could spruce up your rotten life, and
Rejuvenate your abandoned dreams!

Now clear my ways, Gobaraghati!
Robust vans of the company won't scruple
To trample on your crippled skeletons
If it can glorify India, making her
The crown of the world, at the expense
Of your paternal soil, and
Human dignity."

A Word on the Horizon

Someone scripted a word
On the horizon;
Weaponry boasting about
Ended up or the wars that have not yet begin
Stood humbled up before it,
Venomous vipers buried hoods, while
Invectives of dastardly demons
Got transformed into hymns.
What's the word, now?

The whole world was drowned
In the depth of darkness
Reflecting ignorance,
Morning star slumbered
Like an atheist's faith, at dawn;
Morning slackened its onset
As feeble remnants
Of life before death.

Someone scripted a word
Upon the hill…
Clouds heading for deserts
Turned back sprouting hopes,
Barrens bulged with bliss, and
Calves ran after cows
Making rapid grunts.

High tides kept submerging the banks,
Fisher folk with boats in deep seas
Hadn't veered away
From clutches of storm,
The warning letter still lied
Beside the dead body;
No one knows but
Someone scripted a word
On the wet banks-
Cadres holding hostage went slack,
Daggers raised for slaughter
Began composing love letters,
Truculent nations erased boundaries
Embracing humanity.

Ravenous locusts hadn't ceased
Feasting in the corn fields,
Beheaded performers dancing unscarred
Even before the gun points,
Dice game of Hastina
Still being played at Niyamgiri,
The gang-raped schoolgirl
Hadn't come to her senses:
Someone scripted a word
On cloud edges-
Siblings vying for the hidden treasure
Suddenly grew magnanimous.
Dynamite could no more blast the rocks,
As the moon began to climb the sky,
Rhythm of tinkles
Came back to the ankle-bells,
The procession disappeared into oblivion

Leaving land, water and shade
At their own ambits.

Whoever He may be, but
He scripted a word
On the void…

What could be that word?
A few went pondering;
Some speculated it an 'illusion',
Others accepted it as 'Mother.'

■

Kandulana

She plucked flowers from plants,
Spread them over winnowing fan
Under dewy night sky,
Collected grass from hill slopes,
Berries and leaves from the grove;
For tomorrow's Akshay Tritiya:
The day to worship the Mother Earth.

On her way back from school
Through jungles Kanduli recollects
The tales grandpa narrates
Of tigers, forests and men
To induce sleep into her tender eyes;
The frocks that nuns donated her
Are all torn; she'll seek money
From Grandpa for her frocks...

There's a lone berry tree
On her way back through the jungle;
Exhausted, she often sits underneath,
Recollects with wistful eyes
The pale face of her father, now dead.

Everything, except the tree,
Seems rushing at her

With bows and arrows,
Grandpa also has a bow;
Someone from the tumultuous wind
Seemed to shout at her
"Run away, Kandulana!
Run away!"

With frowning face she taunts:
"Why should I run away from grandpa?
He harbours a heaven in his heart for me.
An empathic moon shines there
Dispelling our darkness;
People visiting us from cities
Capture us in camera, and
Adore our love…"

Kanduli misses her grandma
As she reaches home, but finds
A ladle of rice-gruel, and a fistful
Of fried spinach
Kept in an earthen pot for her.
She manages, but dreams
Of the promise made to them:
The KBK that hangs only in posters
On office walls will shine soon
To transform their lives.

Grandpa brandished an axe,
Fire in his eyes…
Kanduli could sense for a moment
A chopping sound before it engulfed her being.
"Human blood pleases the Mother Earth"-
Used to say the old man as Kanduli listens

With no attention; but today,
Her blood would stir up
A million stars and the soul of her father.

Rice soaked in her warm blood
Will be offered as fistful- Akshi,
The land will celebrate the day
Amid fertile fervor; but
No one can ever more see
The little Kandulana again.

(Berenika Kandulana, a ten-year-old girl was sacrificed by her grandfather Rajesh Hembram on April 27, 2009 to mark Akshi Trutiya.)

Naxalite Girl

The most macabre leaders
Stand awestruck in the camp
Like the stilly summer trees;
Younger cadres are dumb with displeasure;
For tears have rolled down
The cheeks of the Naxalite girl.
Won't Naxals look human
If ever they weep?

She frolicked in her childhood
Stamping white ants' hills,
Trampling ants in queues, and
Clipping wings of dragonflies.
Dad teases her with a grin:
"My daughter is fit to be a Naxal
When she grows up…"
Mom calls her fondly a tomboy…
Stirring the whirlwind of time
She conquers all hurdles, and
And dons eye patches; and finally
Turns Naxalite.

Trainers command her
To look down to the soil, not
Upward at the sky,

For the sky lured one with
Clouds, dreams and fairies…
She cannot now reminisce her past
As it treasured lullabies of infancy,
Tales of the cow pardoned by panther,
Prayers soaked in devotion,
Lonely rustle of leaves, and
Murmur of bees.
All these are forbidden for a Naxal;
Pity and compassion: taboos.

The Naxal girl has turned nostalgic
With the hypnotic calls
Of the woodpecker;
Sketched on soil
The face of her friend, Sudha;
And, wished to free
The caged pigeons.

Pull her into the torn marquee
Reminding her of her branded back
And inhuman torment of gulping
The leftover rice in alloy-faded platter
Of aluminum,
Before human sentiment overpowers her.
Inflame her with the tale of the kin
Who outraged her modesty, and
Injured her with a sickle
In a city inn before going elusive.

Entrap the Naxalite girl
Before she turns human

Train her in primitive cruelty,
Savagery and rancor
Before she turns the gentle breeze of Spring
Or the rhythmic warble of rain,
Electrify her, embolden her
Like a Tsunami or a cyclone!

Immersion

The city dazzled
With Her divine splendor
As she ascended the street pandal
Bedecked with pearl white laces.
Her agile feet on the leaping lion,
Seductive locks of hair
Scattered across the direful chest
Of the lascivious demon.

Eyes
Expansive as horizon
Had gathered in them
Century-old sunrises and sunsets;
Her celestial crown
Crafted with mortal ego
Undiminished even after
Famines, war, 'n' calamities;
A slice of sardonic smile
Made up of desolate dark-moon
Hung from her thirsty lips.

The platter for worship
Lacks something eternally
Whatever offering you may adorn it with,
Imploring to the innocent kid of goat
For a palm full of blood-
She has all the while been impatient
From the beginning of her worship.

As she descended on earth-
Meadows exulted with dancing Kans grass,
Thirty-three crore deities
Invoked her with humility,
Her bamboo-sheath glittered
With weapons offered to her,
Tumultuous sky stormed upon the earth
Shattered at her shriek.

She'd inflamed, being the holy grass
The dying wick in the sluggish nerves;
Turning clothes into alluring clouds
She flew them into endless skies.

She's all sins; all prayers incarnate…
She's all enemies; paragon of amour…
She's the Death; and she's all Creation…
She's Invocation, and she's Immersion…

The wee hours today shall
Witness the immersion…

The city has returned with tiresome feet
After the whole night's dance,
Fond memories of all clamour
Vanished into thin air…
Straw lion, straw demon and straw Goddess
Embrace each other
In the river waters today…
And, the sullen moon alights
The vacant pandal of the Goddess!

Today is the Rally

A protest rally will delay
Departure of Falaknamah train
Predicted a traveler while
Boarding Talcher-Puri passenger…
Five-year-old kid asked his father
"What's 'rally' dad?"
Rally is a monster's name.
Monster? Must be huge?
Is it bigger than a hill?
"Yes, I think so," says the man.
Is it bigger than sky too?
Yes.

What about its eyes?
It's like a lake; teeth like trees.
He laughs like a blast!

Where does he stay?
He hides in the crooked,
Rotten skulls of politicos.

When does he come out, dad?
He is out during Assembly session,
Or when voters forget party
Or politicians.

Son asks: What does Rally eat then?
Yes, he eats pan cake, *dalma*, traffic,
Platform, temple and mosque,
Currency, wages and transport vehicles.

Dad, why don't you kill it?
I want to finish it, by plucking
Hair-strand of his life,
But I don't know which strand to pick;
I don't know, how.

Diary of a Betel-Vineyard Farmer

These brats teach Satan
How to scare away
Lone walkers in distant
Orchards of darkness:
They aren't ours, children!
They are apparitions of night
In wasteful days.

The tender betel leaf saddens at
The pangs of our hunger, but
These brats never care for us;
The vine-yard bears a desolate look as
Weight of creeper bends its waist;
But these wild loafers don't realise how
Bones creak under strain of hard work.

They are only a bundle of orders
Emanating from red-tapism;
Their soft-words pierce
Like edge of sharp knives.

They've left infancy behind
Far off at borders of their villages,
How would they envisage that

Even Heaven stoops in pity
At sweat-drops of our anguish
A whole life's toil vanishes into nothingness
When we shed our tears of pain.

Let them bulldoze towers
Of our toil – our betel-vine yards,
They have callous hearts for our protests.
They are under orders
To crush the uprising showing no pity
With heart- hard and insensate as rock;
Show them wrists for hand-cuffs,
Prove yourselves unfazed and strong
Concealing the docile rams in you.

Come on kids, let's get back home,
Let's weep all night
Clasping each others' hands,
Remember what Grandpa told us:
The Lord is born out of wailings;
You may not have heard, but
I know it well.

Diary of a Courtesan

A son is a real gold & daughter
an alloy – An adage in Odisha

My loathe body dwells in
Fragrance at nightfall
My tinkle bells get tired
With their protruding teeth
People of position
And connoisseurs of flesh
Sleep long after daybreak
At my house, a harlot's den;
The hand that unfurls Tricolour
Unfastens my under-garments.

Some tipsy youth runs
His fingers through my hair
Whispering: Where is your house?
: Mali Street in Bhubaneswar...
Or Sonagachhi in Bengal.
What's your name?
: It's Jasmine or Dandelion.
Will you marry me?
(The guy looks so anxious!)
Sometimes I say 'Yea', and
Often say 'No'.

I never fall for your trappings
In the crowds or discotheques
Amid laser lights;
I am what I show up,
My lips bear the intoxication
Of all the wars of civilization.

I purify all sinners:
All wayward, wild and ornery
Gather here, at this damned place;
All their blood and sweat
I collect in my hands.

The moth and butterfly
Figure in my garland
I'm a splint in torch
The undercurrent in a storm.

Find my name, zodiac sign from horoscope:
The sparrow may chirp my nickname;
School register may reveal
My village or police station;
But my current address is
Where I live at the moment.

My gates are flaunt open
Even if whole globe shuts its door.

Couplets of Rebellion

Who's that wight other day
Breathed his last,
Time hanging still
In his frail waist.

His head drooped down
In silence endless,
I implored umpteen times
But he lay there wordless.

The dream had still not blossomed
His India had to be parted,
Look here! I bear the scar
Still on my forehead.
Morning joyful with games
No more my own at night,
Why oh! My father- you
Forgot all you wished!

The whole nation slumbered
But wandered he restless,
Woebegone he wept
As though raining through his eyes.

Patriotism he infused
With his clarion call to the nation,

Even children forgot their books
And jumped on to the rebellion.

Like puffed rice
Flung during cremation
Nation gets pushed
Towards hell,
Why does ah! The rising moon
Sink when it should dazzle?

Give me if you can
An inch of Sabarmati,
Don't promise me a paradise
Or lure with property.

I uncaged a dove of peace,
Who turned it into vulture?
Trading arms in disguise
Who's that street vendor?

I mixed milk and jaggery
It turned bitter as neem,
As rats make merry in empty drum—
What a mockery of freedom!

Shame on that Nation

I detest that nation
Whose naked kids sleep
On swampy platforms with
Thin sheets of rag cover-
One patting the younger sibling;
The mother sits staring
With vacant looks skyward.

Shame on the nation
Where starved kids devour in a
Tattered plate some fried rice
With loathsome stray-dogs;
The woman raises the load of stone-chips
To the rugged head of her man, while
The petty contractor stares lustily
At her scantily covered bouncing bosom.

Despise that country where
A little girl's compelled
To quit school, and
Exhibit rope-walking acrobatics-
Her mom tinkles the tambourine
Feeding teats to infant in arms;
Storing the half-puffed roll of tobacco
Through his hairs above the ear

The joyless father picks up
The drum of his livelihood.

Hate that nation where leaders
Emerge in their ironed clothes
Wearing Kanpur slippers
After a blast to pay succour;
Troops wake up to rush
To borders in a war-like euphoria,
Indulged in temptations and games
Even farmers forget to sow seeds.

I despise such a state where
A father molests his own daughter
Where a sacred sandalwood mark
Smells of inebriating date palm juice
And ropes- illusions of serpents.

■

Jhunu Garg

She climbed down
Her office stairs
Up to her sleek limousine
When it drizzled
Through leaves in darkness

Amid illuminating neon lamps
Jhunu Garg comes out
Of her chamber
As her orderly dumps the files
Wrapped in red sack,
Bundling future of nation,
In car dickey.

The middle aged drowsy man
On stool has awakened:
His waist preparing to bend down,
His fingers servile since years
Now ready to salute Jhunu Madam.

Madam may glance around
When she alights stairs
With boastful tulip smiles
Like an exhausted afternoon that
Drops down in silence.

She leaves the secretariat somber,
Her graceful walk sans
Slippers can bloom lilies
On land, her vision without
Spectacles can reflect moon.

Fate of hapless hundreds
Hangs in her shoulder-long locks
Pleas of many destitute before their death
Fall on her ears…
She's just returned from tour of a
Cholera-afflicted terrain.

Her bureaucratic grace humbles
In modesty under minister's clout
Her pink-petalled lips go dry
With servile words from dawn to dusk.
Humans may not, but
The dry trunk, patridges know
Jhunu Madam's compassion
For impoverished commoners
Who have no backing or future.

Ministers beyond reach,
Henchmen on indolent beach-
Jhunu Madam feels trapped like a bird.
As dew drops on lotus petals-
Perspiration accumulate
On her wide forehead

What a spectacle is that
Under tree amidst jungle?
Land soaks warm blood,

Clipped wings of hens nearby,
Cream juice in clay bowl,
Littered grass blades and vermilion!

Madam removes her glasses,
Looks back; someone cries:
Sorcery!
 No Madam; it's witch worship.
 Locals indulge in; yes Madam, it's so.

Ritual? She reacts cautiously pretending a shock:
Wow, what a wonderful way!
A deadwood may turn into
Minstrel in this part of world.
(Thanks to cholera outbreak)

Jhunu Madam moves on
To explore bed-ridden nation
Despondent under
Septuagenarian flag;
Not a drop to drink,
Its hair disheveled
Like chatter boxes
In naked embodiments
Whose ballot papers
Bear stamp of indelible ink.

Jhunu Garg drafts report
"We've given away rehydration
Solutions; sprinkled bleaching
Into every pit, puddle
And rivulet,
Attention drawing hoardings

Denying cholera deaths,
Statistics showing figures..."

She settles in her comfy
Office vehicle and
Her saree border shine
Feebly in the headlamps for the last time...
Humble salutations
Of afflicted democracy were
Getting dragged
In the mirror of her sedan!!

Tsunami-1

Reminiscences overwhelm my heart
As I recollect you all
On the New Year eve, today.

I'd otherwise recall tonight,
Some younger day pranks, or
Remember rare lines
From love letters of my beloved, or
Some egotistical officer
Who'd embarrassed me a lot;
But, nothing that sort happened.

The night preceding your departure
Some of you got
The luggage ready when
Men sipped tea leisurely
In their drawing rooms
Reminding you to pack kids' stockings,
Caps and winter garments in.

Some of you kept yourselves busy
Listing out errands and destinations,
Some sent e-mail to the son in Jordan,
Some of you cautioned

The family members you left behind
To keep doors bolted all day and night.

And finally, you departed
Waving hands through the wind shields,
With wistful looks at the basil altar,
Flower vase and birds perching
On phone cables,
You exulted at the beauty
Of your country.
Hills, streams and wayside trees
Bade farewell like beloved kin
While the horizon kept moving ahead
Refusing to depart from you.

Many of you had settled there
From the beginning
Offered prayers at churches
Each New Year eve;
Lighting holy sticks of ritual
You've invoked your ancestors
Who are now gathered among stars;
In foggy nights under moon beams
You've talked to angels stealthily.

But, you never returned
To that home, where
You had left behind your fond memories,
Tiny tear drops and fragile dreams
Puerile scorn and generous affection;
Never bothered to remember
Whose boats are moored at jetties.

Newspapers couldn't trace
Your whereabouts at hotels,
Went back from your slums:
You became the headlines
In the wee hours!!

Tsunami: 2

I cannot recollect anything today
Except haunting memories of yours,
Cannot forget rave midnight parties
You've left in some distant islet;
The mehndi-decorated palm
You've patted on your son's back
While sleeping him in your lap;
The coral necklace you'd wished
But could never buy
At the tribal fair;
Still remember how you heaved sighs into
Depths of ocean in darkness.

Why do I reminisce about you?
Are you all my kinsmen?
Why do your palms and ankles
Flash before my eyes amid the
Feeble light of crackers
Fired to welcome the New Year?

Were you my school buddies
Who recited prayers
At assembly along corridor
Many centuries ago?
Were we the ones that broke-up

After that first crush
When the missive you'd written stealthily
Got unveiled under bamboo bushes?
Didn't I fetch you colourful
Kite and snake balloon
From Ladukeswar fair
As I had promised?

But you all left us
Breaking all bonds.

I could've met you this year
Perhaps at a poets' night in Port Blair,
You'd seem very close to my heart
Even though I've never seen you beforehand,
May be I would gather you in my lap
Wiping away your tears while
You're lost at some festival
In Puri or at Konark,
Or while looking for your son
Lost in the banks of the Ganges-
I could call you from your back;
"Dad! Oh my daddy!"

A cursed year it was: alas!
You were swept away in tsunami.

Wind suffused with your sweet humming
Used once to enthrall us all;
But you're a mere memory today-
Nothing more than a dumb sand-art
In the eternal void of nothingness.

When you are already gone-
Rest there in peace;
Do not look back in bewildered eyes
From hill-tops or milky ways.

Kin of your insentient past-
We swear we'll salute
Each of your terrified footprints
Left indelible on this holy soil.
Only your memories obsess the mind now:
This is the maiden night
Of the coming New Year.

∎

Missing Village

Not a single soul was there to tell
Why they had deserted the village
Burying faces amid
Torn pages of history like the
Snake-charmer's rat hiding in a basket
Scared at the mention of the one
It's forbidden to face up.

The Satan no more was there
To obstruct the way of the village priest
Coming home in mid-night
From a distant fair;
Vultures hid themselves
Becoming engraved letters on the
Palm leaf manuscripts of country rituals.
Goddesses sauntering whole village
Through the night had sheltered
In contractor's temple
Blowing out their divine light.

Just as my boyhood days
Vanished becoming kisses planted on
Blushing cheeks of a maiden-
Village no more lived there in the village.
As there were no banyan trees

Darkness no more reigned there;
Without darkness no ghosts were found,
With ghosts disappeared whatever fear was there, and
Sans fear- not a God was there.

Morning, noon and sunset
Had leagued together
To desert the village
Along with all dragonflies and butterflies
Before the moon climbed up the sky
Slumber set in
Listless lay the village street
After defeat in the election
With the gamchha wrapped around head
Grandpa had disappeared
Among somber clouds
Shelving remnants of his belief
In his loincloth.

The village was no more like a village.
It now dazzled on the
Sharp edges of daggers
In the moonlit night
Imploring for an Indira Awaas
Through an obscure petition!!

Nickname For a Daugther

Toying with his paper-boat
The son asks mom with innocent fancy:
"Are there more boys or more girls
In our country, Maa?"

Dithering for a moment
Mom recounts sadly how
People kill their baby girls
Pouring venom into their mouths
Soon after they are born.

Unaware of worldliness and sorrow
The poor child enquires;
'Soon after birth? Or they let her grow
Until a few months old?"
Mom replies
Gulping down her unseen tears
"They are all doomed to die
Soon after they are born."

Floating in rainwater
The small paper boat
He sighs deep, and asks again;
"Why do they do so, Maa?

Why don't they let girls grow
And allow them to play?
Do they ever name the girls or not?"

"Oh, no!" replies the mother,
Holds her son in embrace, and
Reflects with an anguished heart:
"Could anyone ever descry her teardrops
Before they soaked into
The agonized soil,
When a woman had to
Kill the mother in her
Before poisoning her own daughter?
She must have dreamt
A name for her daughter, and
Called her by that name
In her solitary hours.
She alone knows the name."

The Matter Is...

She isn't keen on anything,
She's earned herself the trouble,
She won't heed wise counseling
She'd lie on bed, stay slothful
Keep on eating like glutton

Annoyed? She'll stay hot headed
Weeping? She'll keep sobbing.

What's the matter with your
Daughter-in-law? asked
The lady doctor.

Nothing. It's her eccentricities.
She'd devour watered rice
If you forbid, she'd take a dip
If you warn her against bathing
She'd fast if you tell her to eat
You can't tackle her
Your advice will fall
On her deaf ears
She complains of migraine
Before cocks crow
And retch by sunset.

She broods sitting silent,
Her mom-in-law pondering:
You've servants and maids
You've nothing to do here
Will you listen? Go, take a while
Recline on the divan...

Sleep, prescribes the physician.
Sleep? Did you say sleep?
That's what she always does,
Won't budge even if you wake her up
Short-tempered she is
So unpredictable, complains
The mother-in-law.

Headache in the morning?
Daughter-in-law says 'No'
Do you take food on time?
Yes, she responds weakly
Looking once at mother-in-law, and
Then down at the earth.

Heavy work at home?
Not at all, she says looking skyward
Wanna meet parents?
No, she says.
And menstrual periods?
Regular. Occasional delays.

Take a capsule twice daily,
Tablet thrice daily
Take syrup at bedtime
And see me next month.

She gets up as her mother-in-law
Embraces her reassuringly:
She's like my own daughter, not son's wife;

As her veil drops down
Lo! There's a red stain on her
Tender cheek...
What's the scar, auntie? asks the doctor
Where is it? Fumbles the mother-in-law.

The young woman turns to her
Physician as she goes in,
Just as a lost country-dream
Follows spellbound
The call of some deity,
Just as a slice of Id moon
Settles down in
Distant horizons...

Rain-Drenched

Who knocked the door
At this nocturnal hour?

It's thunderbolts and showers
Overshadowing moon, stars, Earth
Watering down slushy lanes
When someone bangs
Your door at this hour!

I opened the middle latch
Without waking up anyone;
In the drizzling night
Someone stood under porch,
Her form revealed for a while
In the lightning;
Dangled like a bunch of grapes
Her disheveled wet hair
Upon temple and shoulders;
Forehead smeared with vermillion
Like China rose thrown away after worship,

Her eyeballs cold
Like the waters of a still lake
Covered under a thick blanket of fog,
Her lips sealed as though

She'd never before smiled
Or muttered words.
Urdu script tattooed
On her right arm as she'd lost
Her hand down elbow,
Her saree soiled with mud and blood
No crown atop her head.

Drowned in hopes and fears
I asked her after a moment's dither:
"Who're you, Maa?
What brings you here
At this hour of night?"

Gesturing at dirt-filled cobwebs, and
Moth eaten map on the wall she said:
"You forgot my name
And identity within years!
I am the village".
I realised, she's no other than
My Mother Earth where I learned
To crawl: My India.
"Yes, you are my mom!"
I caught hold of her feet, and wept.

What more?
What could you ask your mother
At this hour of night
In such a plight?

I whisked her into the drawing room, and
Sat her on a wooden chair,
My tears had washed

Mud stains off her feet,
I wrapped around her
A clean khadi Tri-colour
To be unfurled by some Minister
The next morning.

Was it the same Mother
Who had tied toys in her veil
For kids who never came home
Back from school...till today.

A Son's Letter to Father

My regards, Dad,
Grandpa is bed-ridden
And Mom is praying:
How do you do Dad?
What are they doing with you?

Do they offer you bread
And black tea for breakfast?
What do you have at supper?
I suppose hot rice for lunch;
Do they give you rope cot
Like we've one at home?

Do they call you Antaryami*
By your name? What names
They are known by
Other than 'terrorists'?

Are they cowards like rats and mongoose?
Why aren't they familiar
Faces in streets 'n' slums
If they aren't coward?
Why are they hiding in forests
Abducting men from homes
And towns, like hyena stealing
Calves from pen or otter

Snatching chicken from
Puddle embankment?

Do you think they are patriots, papa?
But they are, says my chum Jaffer's father.
Why couldn't I see such heroes then
In textbooks of history,
Or find their portraits
On our school corridor?

Were they patriots-
They would look commanding
Like Mahatma Gandhi, or
Resplendent as Netaji
Carrying rose petals, not
Pistols in their trousers,
And who're these fellows Dad?

Don't they have a hearth under a roof?
Didn't they catch butterflies
In their childhood?
Haven't they built castles
Of sand on wet banks
Of river or haven't they flown
Kites; haven't they wept alone
In mango groves?

Don't they have a home,
A country or a name?
Who'll buy me Tri-colour flags
When you aren't home?
If at all they kill you tomorrow,
Who'll back our naked lives?

The Prime Minister's speech
From ramparts of Lal Quilla
Will stun the nation, when
He'll unfurl flag in sky;
The crimson coloured towel
You bought from local market
May be on your shoulders;
Why did you build a nest
In that Goddamned nation
Where you can't live in peace
Let alone save a soul?

Would do God-
You come back home, papa,
Safe with life;
Mom is praying, and
Grandpa is bedridden!

■

(*Antaryami, an Indian driver, was held hostage by Iraqi abductors.)

Tribute to Hetal

Birds retreat to nest at dusk
From distant hutments,
Familiar street-vendors retire
To slums with vending-baskets,
After ferrying the whole day
Boats are back to the dock,
The wayward God
Dragged back for prayers,
Classmates return from school
Except Hetal alone!

You are all back home,
"Where's Hetal?" Wondered Mom,
The flower plant said:
I saw her at dawn;
Teacher said she was in games,
Birds said they're at pains singing:
Home is where love stays
It feels good to leave home
It feels better to get back home;
Stars whispered to each other, but
It could never be heard through the winds.

The one who comes back
Other day was not Hetal.

Who is she then?
She didn't have anklets
Her Mom had bought,
Red ribbon on her hair
Her pink-coloured frock
With blood stains on her groin,
Her dried up tears reflected
A gloomy afternoon:
Dad said it's over,
And Mom wondered:
"What's this, Oh my Mom!"

It's not a matter of long past, Hetal!
You'd have looked resplendent
With vermillion on your forehead;
Cheerful like mango fruition
In bunches with humility;
Your gracious bridal walk
Would remind spring tides;
Lifeline on your palms
Was full of assurances.
It's not a matter of long past, Hetal!

You emerge spreading your palms
From the darkness of distant hills,
But we send you back each night
Unable to fill them with justice:
"Come later, not today, Hetal" we console, but know
You'll never return to ask anything.
Your tender palms will be overflowing
With the blood of the vulture that
Devoured your virgin green adolescence.
Unlike your earlier slothness

You'll appear glaring tomorrow
As indelible calendar ink.

You'll wear again regular school tunic
Tomorrow on August fifteen,
And red ribbon on your plait
Like azure horizon at dawn.
Your nestling beaks will glow again;
Everyone will search for you;
"Where is Hetal" the teachers will enquire
Each one in the mass
Will hear you sing National Anthem,
An invisible hand will carry
A packet of sweetmeat
To an unending desolation
Unseen, and in silence.

Two shadows will return
From gallows with sighs
Into remote villages
Where no one will light up
A lamp for worship at sunset;
Not only your mother, but
The whole nation will
Stare at the sight.

Speak up, Hetal!
Are these tears for you alone?

(Hetal Parekh was a school student of Bankura district of West Bengal who was sexually assaulted and killed on March 5, 1990. Accused Dhananjoy Chatterjee, 39, was executed on August 14, 2014)

No-Devakee

Friends and countrymen!
I may don any role
Except the one
Of a mother; Never.

I'll have to cook lunch at dawn
Before cocks crow,
Catch bus on schedule
In downtown transport
Hanging like crowded bats
From gummy steel rods,
And reach stuffy office
Like lame cockroaches
To grind files all day.

Boss back in office
Post late lunch recollects
Urgent dictation to summon:
"Debina, need to take note now".

Attendance register gets
Scruffy with more cross marks,
Dirty smiles dangles like smut
From lips of the head clerk,
Non-drawable provident fund
Show-causes from top brasses,

Future getting crippled
Under burden, like a tortoise-
They queue up all mocking at me
In my dreams.

Do not trap me with sophistry
I know your cunningness:
You creep stealthily
To tickle my tired feet
Clear my drooping locks
Off the corners of eyes,
Fancying my shrinking body
As acquiescence, you'll unhook
The shying outfit at my back, and
Command me to become a mother; but
When I prepare myself to become a mom
You leave me dispassionate
Rejoicing at your victory.

Tying up saree around the waist
I've to draw water from an abysmal well,
All alone, bring down hefty cauldron
Of boiled rice from smoky hearth,
Seek amid distant stars in the sky
Lullabies now forgotten, and
Invoke moon to induce sleep;
All alone by myself.

I alone will move restless
Like gudgeon writhing on inflamed oven
If ever kids are late from school;
Find leisure to learn weaving sweater
From the unfriendly neighbor!

Auspicious moment of giving birth
Is God's grace;
I'll never bother
If at all it's delayed...
Even if I don't become a mother
Or become something else.

I wouldn't hesitate to become a mother, but
How would I give suck to the baby, for
I've mortgaged my breasts and nipples
With large companies for advertisement;
How would I catch
Dragonflies for my kids, as
I've left my slender fingers
Amid cold insensate key-boards;
How would I put kajal(collyrium) on my kids, when
I've lost the container to the crows?
When would I feed my kids, and
Lull them with my love?
My mornings are not my own, just as
My evenings are slaves to others.

Nithari

You can listen at every door
Mid-day or late at night
An elder imploring:
"Do not bother me, my child,
Hear the cricket creak,
It'll take you away,
Nithari is around!"

Who is Nithari?
Is it a man, home or a town
None can say who it is!

He may have abandoned
Bones he couldn't grind
With his devilish teeth,
Samples may be found
Around sewerage ditches
From hospital dumps
Labs can guess age or gender
Of bones, but none can recall
Their history!

Smart television or newspapers
Reveal clues with alert messages:

Someone lures kids from school ground
With chocolate or kites,
Kids half-asleep or on their way to school
Are carried away into dingy caves
Where candles flicker
With the fear of darkness.

Nithari looks like sheen
Of a bloodied knife used
In a brutal killing,
His breathing sounds coarse, and
Hiccups smells like
Fermented date palm juice
After sun rise,
His eyes are wild
Like the ones of demons living in story books
Time has christened it as Nithari.

Nithari with his little dress sense
Doesn't like clothing up,
With his virility hanging below his waist
Like a battery discharged torch-
He swings kids
Closing their eyes in terror, and
Compels them to sing;
"Recite!" he'll scream and chop off
Their tongue as they sing;
"Dance!" he'll command,
And will remove calf muscles
As they begin to dance;
Forces kid to pose as cows
Before stabbing them with his horns.

When he fold his hands,
You won't remember God, but
His blood-thirsty dazzling axe;
Chirping of birds and gurgling
Of streams; exuberance of giggles
Or heart-rending tears
Cannot ever shake Nithari.
When he spills, lakes turn red
When he flies entire sky
Gets into delirium
With stench of his virile fluid.

Nithari hangs on all day
Over heaps of black berries
Pecked by bats until sunset;
He neither smiles nor rejoices
How can kids ascertain
The secret strands of his life!!

Imrana, For You...

Moon plays hide 'n' seek
Under floating clouds;
Your hands sans bangles
Emerge from decrepit papers;
A storm is brewing!

What's the time now?
: It's the wee hour.
Imrana shut her eyes
But she isn't asleep,
A tiger growl is drowning
At close quarters
Of her Nikahnamah.

Wish, I wake you up
Imrana, amidst solitary nights;
Invite you for a stroll
Into the gardens
We'll sit on sand dunes
And gossip for hours.

What shall we talk Imrana
When all those episodes are over?
What's this under your naqaab?
Tears and sighs!

Where did you go Imrana?
You never let me know.

Was there no one around
When the old pet tiger
Prowled in your bedroom?
Didn't you have a glass bangle on wrist
To make it a knife against the beast?
Or a tooth on your gums
To use as a weapon?

I know, your man had gone
To workplace; mom-in-law away;
Kids busy playing dice and counters at a distance
Your scream couldn't reach; but
No one else heard your screams?

What were Gods doing then?

Was God listening to prayers;
Siva engrossed in smoke
Of camphor, or Allah
In holy sync with His kids
Offering Namaj
When the tiger sucked your teats?
Or licked your mound
Of Venus in public?

Ditching humans decrepit as crab-shells
For tigers hungry and uncaged
Countrymen have retired to slumber;
Naxal-friends began writing slogans
For rebellions of tomorrow;

The lord turned up with lusty smiles
To fondle buttocks of the barmaid;
Cab driver Chaita-
Carefree as a weaver bird
Went off to the bar as he does every day
After a whole day's work;
Only I buried my face in shame.

In my shame sank through the earth
The desolate lonely Sita
Sans witness for her chastity.

Come out Imrana!
I stretch out the Grand Arms of poetry:
I'm no Yadav, neither a cleric:
I 'm neither a man nor a woman!

www.ingramcontent.com/pod-product-compliance
Lightning Source LLC
Chambersburg PA
CBHW031125080526
44587CB00011B/1113